STRATEGIC PLANS, JOINT DOCTRINE

AND ANTIPODEAN INSIGHTS

Douglas C. Lovelace, Jr.
and
Thomas-Durell Young

October 20, 1995

* * * * * *

The authors of this essay would like to express their
sincere gratitude to the following individuals for their
insightful and helpful comments made on earlier drafts of
this essay: Dr. William T. Johnsen; COL D.J. Murray, CSC; Dr.
Douglas Johnson; Professor Mike Morin; and COL Phil Mock,
USA, (Ret). Special thanks are accorded to the Directing
Staff of the Australian Defence Force Warfare Centre who
graciously hosted a visit by T. Young, which was sponsored by
the Australian Defence Studies Centre of the Australian
Defence Force Academy, Canberra.

* * * * * *

Comments pertaining to this report are invited and
should be forwarded to: Director, Strategic Studies
Institute, U.S. Army War College, Carlisle Barracks, PA
17013-5050. Comments also may be conveyed directly to the
authors by calling commercial (717) 245-4058/3010 or DSN 242-
4058/3010,or via Internet at lovelacd@carlisle-emh2.army.mil.

FOREWORD

This is the second in an analytical series on joint issues. It follows the authors' *U.S. Department of Defense Strategic Planning: The Missing Nexus*, in which they articulated the need for more formal joint strategic plans. This essay examines the effect such plans would have on joint doctrine development and illustrates the potential benefits evident in Australian defense planning.

Doctrine and planning share an iterative development process. The common view is that doctrine persists over a broader time frame than planning and that the latter draws on the former for context, syntax, even format. In truth the very process of planning shapes new ways of military action. As the environment for that action changes, planners address new challenges, and create the demand for better methods of organizing, employing and supporting forces. Evolutionary, occasionally revolutionary, doctrinal changes result.

The authors of this monograph explore the relationship between strategic planning and doctrine at the joint level. They enter the current debate over the scope and authority of joint doctrine from a joint strategic planning perspective. In their view, joint doctrine must have roots, and those roots have to be planted firmly in the strategic concepts and plans developed to carry out the *National Military Strategy*. Without the fertile groundwork of strategic plans, the body of joint doctrine will struggle for viability.

The Strategic Studies Institute offers this analysis with the aim of stimulating further dialogue about our system of developing joint doctrine and joint strategic plans.

RICHARD H. WITHERSPOON
Colonel, U.S. Army
Director, Strategic Studies
    Institute

PRECIS

The relationship of strategic planning for the U.S. armed forces to the development and implementation of joint doctrine is opaque, but important. Strategic plans, by translating the *National Military Strategy* into strategic concepts, could guide the development and implementation of joint doctrine. This essay identifies the many improvements that would accrue to the joint doctrine development process, as well as to the implementation of joint doctrine, if the Chairman of the Joint Chiefs of Staff were to develop strategic plans, as defined herein. Strategic concepts, derived from strategic plans, would provide a basis for the development of joint doctrine, thus ensuring joint doctrine is more responsive to the *National Military Strategy (NMS)*. These strategic concepts, in contrast to those broad concepts found in the *NMS* and other strategic planning documents, would be specific and focused. The linkage of strategic planning and joint doctrine development is not without precedence: the Australian defense planning system has evolved in recent years with the objective, *inter alia*, of producing a useful body of joint doctrine. The Australian Defence Force has been using a planning process by which strategic direction is converted into Strategic Concepts, which form the basis for Australian joint doctrine.

KEY FINDINGS

• Strategic plans should be developed that further define the *National Military Strategy* and provide supporting strategic concepts. These concepts could provide the basis for the development of joint doctrine.

• The practice of Lead Agent in the development of joint doctrine should be modified and the Joint Warfighting Center should be given responsibility and authority for managing the development of joint doctrine.

• Joint doctrine, in accordance with the Chairman's policy, should be universally accepted as authoritative.

• The development of strategic plans can improve adherence to, and implementation of, joint doctrine.

STRATEGIC PLANS, JOINT DOCTRINE
AND ANTIPODEAN INSIGHTS

Introduction.

Over the past decade, "jointness" has become a paean in the quest to improve the effectiveness of the U.S. armed forces, and justifiably so. Recent military operations have demonstrated a high correlation between joint operations and success on the battlefield. Consequently, the trend toward increased "jointness" is not likely to abate. The congressional perception of the importance of joint operations by the U.S. armed forces was underscored by the passage of the 1986 Goldwater-Nichols Department of Defense Reorganization Act ("Goldwater-Nichols Act"), the most significant reorganization and redistribution of authority and responsibilities within the Department of Defense since 1958.[1] In an effort to assure more effective joint operations, Congress increased the powers of the combatant Commanders-in-Chief (CINCs), made the Chairman of the Joint Chiefs of Staff (CJCS) the principal military advisor to the National Command Authorities (NCA), and assigned the CJCS specific responsibilities in the areas of strategic planning, joint training and joint doctrine. Additionally, the Joint Chiefs of Staff lost their baronial influence and the Joint Staff was reoriented to serve the CJCS, vice the corporate Joint Chiefs of Staff.[2]

This does not suggest that this seminal legislation has overcome all the institutional impediments to raising, training and employing joint forces. Problems remain; one of which is the focus of this essay. Difficulties in the development and implementation of sound joint doctrine have been caused, in large measure, by the systemic gap in the existing strategic planning process. The absence of a direct link between the strategic direction of the U.S. armed forces and the operational planning for their employment has hindered the development of coherent and integrated joint doctrine. Also, this situation has not provided effective incentives for the services to embrace joint doctrine, in total. These limitations point to a common solution. They illuminate a missing link in strategic planning for the U.S. armed forces that would connect the *National Military Strategy (NMS)*[3] to key joint planning documents. Filling this strategic planning void would enhance the development and implementation of sound and comprehensive joint doctrine. In short, there is a need for a coherent, traceable, and accountable connection between the *NMS* and the body of joint doctrine developed to support it.

Specifically and proximately, there are no national-level strategic concepts set forth in strategic plans to guide the development and implementation of joint doctrine.[4] Consequently, the current body of joint doctrine can, at best, be only loosely connected to the *NMS*. The development of strategic plans would permit strategic guidance, as first expressed in the form of the *National Security Strategy (NSS)*[5] and then by the *NMS*, to be better conveyed to the service chiefs and the CINCs.

As strategic guidance and direction work their way through the system, they are further refined and defined. This elucidating process should provide specific guidance for the development of a body of more useful and accepted joint doctrine to guide the conduct of operations for U.S. forces, as well as to rationalize the required types, number, and balance of service forces. A process that integrates strategic planning with joint doctrine development would better actualize the intent of the Goldwater-Nichols Act. And, in this era of penury, such reforms would assist the NCA in validating to the Congress that a more effective and efficient national defense capability is being pursued.

While this essay may seem fairly critical of joint doctrine, the process by which it is developed, and the effectiveness of its implementation; one must recognize that the U.S. armed forces have made great progress in developing and promulgating joint doctrine since passage of the Goldwater-Nichols Act. As demonstrated during operations Desert Shield and Desert Storm, the availability and application of joint doctrine have significantly improved the warfighting capabilities of U.S. forces. The purpose of this essay, therefore, is to show how joint doctrine can be further enhanced by eliminating some imperfections in the process by which it is developed, and how more complete implementation can be encouraged. Both can be accomplished by more directly linking joint doctrine to the *NMS*.

The Chairman is aware of two significant problems regarding joint doctrine. First, he is uncomfortable with the level of understanding of joint doctrine within the U.S. armed forces. Recent initiatives, such as the creation of the Joint Warfighting Center and its charge to broaden service understanding of joint doctrine, manifest his concern.[6] Second, he has inferred that the services may not feel obligated to adhere to joint doctrine. This has resulted in his recent direction to the Joint Staff to change the qualifier that appears in all joint doctrine publications from, "This publication is authoritative but not directive..." to "The guidance in this publication is authoritative; as such, commanders will apply this doctrine . . . except when exceptional circumstances dictate otherwise."[7] However, what may be the most important step toward improving the development and implementation of joint doctrine has yet to be taken.

In order to address the problem of the need to improve joint doctrine by better linking it to the *NMS*, this essay will frame the argument in the following manner. First, a brief overview of the value of joint doctrine, the Chairman's responsibilities, and joint doctrine's general utility will be presented. Second, imperfections in the existing joint doctrine development process will be addressed. Third, the current process by which the Chairman translates strategic direction into strategic and operation plans will be examined to show how it could be improved to enhance joint doctrine development and encourage adherence. Fourth, the Australian defense planning process will be presented as an illustrative example of an effective strategic planning process, which facilitates the development and implementation of joint doctrine. Fifth, an assessment of U.S. joint doctrine development and implementation will be provided. Finally, proposals will be presented for reforms aimed at improving the relationship between the strategic planning for the U.S. armed forces and joint doctrine development and implementation.

Joint Doctrine: Overview.

Its Value. Over the past several years, the Chairman has formalized the joint doctrine development process in *Joint Publication 1-01*[8] and has promulgated a substantial amount of joint doctrine.[9] More is yet to come. Viewed within the construct that strategy should address "ends, ways and means,"[10] joint doctrine is as important to successful military operations as the *NMS* is to achieving national military objectives. In short, it is the role of joint doctrine to link what must be accomplished to the tools available or required. Thus, joint doctrine should derive from, *inter alia*, the *NMS* and therefore help implement it.[11]

Similar to how the *NMS* rationalizes defense resources with national military objectives at the strategic level, joint doctrine guides the employment of joint forces and facilitates the use of operational capability to achieve strategic and operational end states. In fact, theater operation plans should be developed to conform to established joint doctrine.[12] It also assists strategic leaders in determining the types and amount of various military capabilities combatant commanders require, as well as ensuring the effective and efficient application of military capability to accomplish specific objectives.[13]

While the value of joint doctrine in improving joint warfighting capability is widely accepted, it also has collateral value. Effective joint doctrine informs senior civilian leadership and governmental agencies as to how they may expect the U.S. armed forces to be employed, and thus illuminates force strengths and limitations. It can also serve a similar purpose for alliance and potential coalition governments and armed forces, particularly apropos establishing a U.S. national position for the development of multinational doctrine.[14]

The Role of the Chairman. The Goldwater-Nichols Act (now codified in *Title 10 of the United States Code [10 USC]*), established a statutory basis for the development of joint doctrine and assigned the responsibility to the Chairman.[15]

Although there is no statutory requirement to do so, each service, to varying degrees, has developed service-unique doctrine. This is not to infer that service doctrine development is unwarranted. It is obviously needed. However, it is clear that Congress recognized the primacy of joint doctrine.

In a broad sense, the Chairman is also responsible for the development of joint training and military education policies for the services.[16] This authority allows the Chairman to influence the nature of joint training in documents such as the *Universal Joint Task List (UJTL)*. It also provides him with opportunities to prescribe how joint training will be evaluated and to influence joint exercises by designating special areas of interest.[17] Within the military education arena, the Chairman can influence the nature and amount of joint education that takes place at service schools.[18] Thus, the Chairman's joint training and military education responsibilities provide additional venues for advancing the implementation of joint doctrine.

Pervasiveness of Joint Doctrine. The utility of joint doctrine extends beyond the employment of joint forces. It affects virtually all of the Chairman's strategic planning activities. Specifically, by combining the responsibilities given the Chairman in sections 153 and 163 of 10 *USC*, one finds he is responsible for soliciting the requirements of the combatant commanders; evaluating, integrating, and establishing priorities; and advising the Secretary of Defense of their requirements, individually and collectively. Additionally, he is to advise the Secretary of Defense on the extent to which service program recommendations and budget proposals conform to the priorities established in strategic plans and for the combatant commanders. This advice may include alternative program recommendations that differ from those submitted by the services.[19]

In integrating and establishing priorities for the requirements of combatant commanders and in assessing service programs, the Chairman logically must consider existing and emerging joint doctrine. Therefore, if elements of service programs do not comport with existing or emerging joint doctrine, the Chairman, as principal military advisor to the

Secretary of Defense and President, may recommend changes to the programs.

The Chairman's triennial report containing recommended changes in the assignment of roles and functions to the services is also influenced by joint doctrine.[20] On the surface this may seem debatable; however, closer examination reveals its validity. A case in point is the proposal by the former Chief of Staff of the Air Force that the battlefield be partitioned and that each section be assigned the responsibility of a service or functional component command. His intent was to assign responsibility for the rear and close "battles" principally to the Army, with the "high" and deep "battles" primarily the responsibility of the Air Force. This proposal, which was inconsistent with joint doctrine, would have called for the transfer of responsibility for close air support to the Army and the responsibility for deep interdiction (currently shared by all services) to become primarily the responsibility of the Air Force, and to a lesser extent, the Navy. Therefore, the Army would be expected to give up its high and deep battle systems, as well as the funding that acquires and maintains them.[21] Given the negative response this proposal received from the "joint community," one may reasonably conclude that any service-initiated changes in roles and functions that do not comport with existing or emerging joint doctrine would not be favorably considered.

Joint doctrine is also crucial for effective joint training and education. It provides the doctrinal principles that orient and focus such training. For example, the UJTL is guided by joint doctrine. Armed with it, joint force commanders perform focused mission analysis and develop Joint Mission Essential Task Lists (JMETL).[22] They can then plan their training programs to meet the requirements of their JMETLs. During the execution of joint training, commanders are able to rely on joint doctrine to frame the broad training tasks and to suggest measures of training effectiveness. The result, obviously, is improvement in joint warfighting capability.

If joint doctrine is patently important and valuable to the national defense, then what can be done to enhance its development and improve its implementation? To answer this question, two areas must be examined: 1) the differing ways the services *themselves* define and perceive doctrine, including their own service doctrine, and 2) the role played by the services in developing joint doctrine. The unique doctrinal orientation which each service brings to the joint doctrine development process provides for valuable, healthy interaction. However, service uniqueness also creates challenges within the process.

Joint Doctrine: Process Imperfections.

Overview. Otto von Bismarck stated: "Laws are like sausages. It is better not to see them being made."[23] Bismarck's analogy seems applicable to the process by which joint doctrine is developed. Joint doctrine is not devised in a manner that necessarily encourages observance, nor does it meet all the expectations and requirements of the services and combatant commands. No less an authority than the current CJCS has stated that joint doctrine ". . . is not well vetted, [not] well understood. It is certainly not disseminated out there, and is almost never used by anyone . . . ." Once these problems are solved, he said "We can go on to the next step and ensure our joint training and joint exercises [are] in consonance with it."[24] Elaborating further on the problem, the Chairman said "I have gone to more joint exercises and walked away [more] embarrassed from them than anything else."[25]

At present, the development of U.S. joint doctrine is a process based upon consensus. Thus, many joint publications reflect the lowest common denominators upon which the services do not disagree.[26] This often results in imprecise, confusing, or contradictory doctrinal concepts. Consequently, internal inconsistencies within the current body of joint doctrine are not uncommon.[27] The key factors contributing to inconsistency in joint doctrine are the differing views of doctrine held by the respective services and the compartmented manner in which it is developed. And, interestingly, an effective vehicle for cross-checking the consistency of various doctrinal publications has yet to be implemented. In a twist of Bismarck's admonition, those who dislike the current doctrinal sausage will better understand why they find it so unappealing after reviewing its development process.

Doctrine: The Services' Views. In an historical sense, the services have not shared similar views as to what "doctrine" *means*, let alone what purpose it should *serve*. The *Miriam-Webster Dictionary* defines doctrine as: "something that is taught, held, put forth as true, and supported by a teacher, a school, or a sect; a principle or position or the body of principles in any branch of knowledge." The Department of Defense's *Dictionary of Military and Associated Terms* (which applies to *all* of the Department of Defense) defines doctrine as: "[f]undamental principles by which the military forces or elements thereof guide their actions in support of national objectives. It is authoritative but requires judgement in application."[28] These definitions notwithstanding, to under- stand the current working definitions of military doctrine, one must examine the varying service perspectives.

Within the Army, doctrine is seen as essential. It is accepted as the basis of the organization as well as the engine of change. It is pervasive, encompassing the Army's ethos, professional qualities, esprit de corps, legal basis, readiness, operations, principles of war and operations other than war.[29] While the Army agrees with the definition of doctrine in the Department of Defense dictionary, it seems to interpret the use of "judgement in application" more liberally than the current Chairman.[30] Army doctrine preceded joint doctrine and the Army's wide experience in the development and use of doctrine has enabled it to be a prime contributor to the ever-growing body of joint doctrine. This has caused one or more of the other services to feel that the Army exerts inordinate influence within the joint doctrine development process.[31] Given the maturity of the U.S. Army's Training and Doctrine Command and the relative inexperience of the doctrine centers of the other services, this is somewhat understandable.

The Navy, notwithstanding its more recent statements to the contrary, has only begun to formalize and institutionalize its own doctrine.[32] The limited emphasis the Navy has historically placed on doctrine can be, at least partially, attributed to its culture, particularly its focus on technology and independent operations. Traditionally, the Navy has viewed doctrine as procedures for applying capital systems. The recently published U.S. Navy's capstone doctrine publication, *Naval Doctrine Publication 1*, lays the foundation for a robust body of doctrine that, nevertheless, has yet to be written, vetted, accepted, and validated. This new publication defines doctrine as being ". . . conceptual—a shared way of thinking that is not directive."[33] The Navy currently believes that doctrine should form a bridge between the *NMS* and the tactics, techniques, and procedures employed by the service.[34] The Navy's acknowledgement of the importance of doctrine notwithstanding, the time required to develop institutional devotion to doctrine and the intellectually vigorous processes necessary for its development will likely extend the growth of a Navy doctrine-based culture well into the future.

The U.S. Air Force defines its doctrine in the introduction of *Air Force Manual 1-1, Basic Aerospace Doctrine of the United States Air Force*. It states,

> Aerospace doctrine is, simply defined, what we hold *true* [emphasis added] about aerospace power and the best way to do the job in the Air Force....doctrine is a guide for the exercise of professional judgement rather than a set of rules to be followed blindly. . . . Doctrine should be alive—growing, evolving, and maturing. New experiences, reinterpretations of former experiences, advances in technology, changes in threats, and cultural changes can all require alterations to parts of our doctrine even as other parts remain constant. If we allow our thinking about aerospace power to stagnate, our doctrine can become dogma.

It appears that the Air Force considers doctrine development and revision to be a more living and fluid process. Its view of doctrine can also be explained in terms of service culture. It results from a predominant focus on technologically advanced systems, and seeks to improve their effectiveness through improved human contributions. As a result, the Air Force believes that one of the defining characteristics of a war is the weaponry employed. The service's lexicon includes system-oriented terminology like "sortie generation," "weaponeering," and "target servicing." The Air Force's focus on systems and its desire to adopt the newest technology results in a focus on system characteristics and the general subordination of doctrine.[35]

The U.S. Marine Corps considers doctrine to be a philosophy of warfighting. Its higher level doctrine does not contain specific techniques and procedures for the conduct of war. Rather, it provides broad guidance in the form of concepts and values. Indeed, a review of *FMFM 1*, *Warfighting*, reveals that Marine Corps doctrine sets forth a particular way of thinking about war and a way of fighting, a philosophy of leading Marines in combat, a mandate for professionalism and a common language.[36] In short, it appears that the Marine Corps views its doctrine as a codification of its essence, its *raison d'être*, rather than a body of knowledge to be consulted in the preparation for, and conduct of, war.

Given this general discussion of service's views of doctrine, it is clear that significant differences exist. It should be noted that service doctrines are developed to meet the unique needs of individual services. The challenge for joint doctrine, on the other hand, is to transcend individual service doctrines, and provide an overarching approach to warfare that effectively integrates each service's contributions. Whereas the development of service doctrines can be accomplished via a bottom-up approach, the development of effective joint doctrine can only be achieved in a top-down manner. A bottom-up approach to the development of joint doctrine can result in nothing more than an imperfect synthesis of the disparate doctrinal bents of the services. A top-down approach, on the other hand, would set forth requisite unifying concepts at the outset. Moreover, joint doctrine is key to the flow of strategic direction that begins with the *NSS*, runs through the *NMS* and strategic plans that contain strategic concepts, and ultimately results in the planning and conduct of operations that support national strategy. Joint doctrine, therefore, should translate strategic concepts into authoritative guidance to the services and the CINCs for the conduct of military operations.

Joint Doctrine: Role of the Services. The current process of developing joint doctrine is limited in its ability to overcome the differing views of doctrine held by the services. Once the Joint Staff's Director for Operational Plans and Interoperability

(J-7) decides on behalf of the CJCS that a new piece of doctrine (Project Proposal) is required, he publishes a Program Directive assigning a Lead Agent to direct the development effort. The Lead Agent, a service in most instances, writes or directs the writing of the drafts of the new publication[37] and is, therefore, able to inject its doctrinal view of the subject area during the early stages of development. The result is that draft joint doctrine may emphasize, early on, what the Lead Agent considers to be its service's unique contributions to the doctrinal issue under consideration. While these parochial views may or may not survive the iterative coordination process unaltered, they establish adversarial relationships among the services. And, the reluctance to raise contentious issues for the Chairman's adjudication may result in doctrine that is not only watered down but also retains a certain amount of bias toward the Lead Agent's service.

The development of joint doctrine can be contentious from the perspective of the services for a different reason. Disagreement exists among the services concerning the actual role to be played by joint doctrine. The U.S. Air Force, for instance, completely agrees with the proviso in *Joint Publication 1-01* that states, "Joint Doctrine will be written to reflect extant capabilities."[38] Thus, from a U.S. Air Force perspective, doctrine development should follow force capability development. That is, technological advances will dictate new or revised doctrine. The Army, alternatively, believes that doctrinal concepts should be more than that and should act as the engine of change, heavily influencing decisions concerning future systems and capabilities.[39] To the extent that there is not a common view of the purpose and utility of joint doctrine and that its development process permits the infusion of service parochialism, the effectiveness of the process is constrained.

Joint Doctrine: Unappetizing Sausages. Criticism of the efficacy of the current joint doctrine development process coupled with the varying views of the purposes and uses of doctrine held by the Chairman and the services tend to cause the latter to not feel bound by joint doctrine, even though it was crafted via a consensus-building process. Furthermore, the ability of the Chairman to direct that doctrine be followed may be viewed as limited since, by law, he is vested with *no* command authority and the Joint Staff is specifically prohibited from exercising any executive authority (i.e, shades of a *Generalstab*).[40]

Yet, the inability to assure uniform application of joint doctrine can have significant negative ramifications. A tragic example is the April 14, 1994 downing of two Army Black Hawk helicopters in Iraq by two Air Force F-15 fighter aircraft, killing all 26 people aboard the helicopters. Recognizing that correct application of joint doctrine may have prevented this tragedy, the Chairman directed "immediate and serious attention" to applicable joint doctrine.[41]

Continued improvement of joint doctrine is required if the U.S. armed forces are to benefit from it as envisaged by the framers of the Goldwater-Nichols Act. Joint doctrine development and implementation problems can be related to incomplete strategic planning. Therefore, it is not surprising that these two problems share a common solution.

Incomplete Strategic Planning.

In theory and practice, joint doctrine should facilitate the implementation of the *NMS*. In *Joint Pub 1*, the Chairman observes that "[t]hough neither policy nor strategy, *joint doctrine* deals with the fundamental issue of how best to employ the national military power to achieve strategic ends."[42] In other words, it should help relate the "ways" to the "means" and "ends." From a purely military perspective, national strategic ends are attained through the accomplishment of military strategic and operational objectives. A key feature of joint doctrine is that it should facilitate the translation of national and theater level strategies into operationally useful methods.

While it is apparent that the *NMS*, in its current form, is of little operational use until it is refracted through the prism of a national military strategic plan, it also seems logical that joint doctrine should be developed to accommodate specific strategic concepts presented in such a strategic plan. The *raison d'être* of the *NMS* is to translate into military terms the

strategic guidance provided by the President's *NSS*. By
design, the unclassified, artistically arranged and widely
distributed *NMS* serves more as a military policy and public
relations document. It communicates the Chairman's views on
the relevancy of military power, as opposed to delving into
the specifics of a strategy designed to achieve specific
objectives.

A review of Section 153, *10 USC* provides some
illuminating information regarding the formulation of
strategic direction and national military strategy and the
development of strategic and contingency plans. This section
describes a hierarchy for strategy development and
promulgation. The first subparagraph charges the Chairman
with the responsibility for assisting the President and the
Secretary of Defense in providing for the strategic direction
of the armed forces.[43] This is, in essence, the purpose of
the *NMS*. Although the *NMS* in its current form is general in
nature, it does provide in broad terms the Chairman's advice
to the NCA regarding the best use of the military element of
power in pursuit of broad national security objectives. The
NMS serves another key purpose; it provides general guidance
to the services, CINCs and defense agencies as to the role
U.S. armed forces will play in achieving national security
objectives.

However, the *NMS* does not provide adequate guidance for
the development of specific objectives, let alone the methods
for attaining them. By its very nature, broad in scope and
general in content, it is open to diverse interpretation.[44]
Consequently, by itself, it is insufficient to guide
effectively the development of, *inter alia*, joint doctrine.
Returning to *10 USC*, the second subparagraph of Section 153
requires the Chairman to "[prepare] strategic plans,
including plans which conform to resource levels projected by
the Secretary of Defense to be available for the period of
time for which the plans are to be effective."[45] These
strategic plans should conform to the *NMS* and carry strategic
direction to a level of increased specificity.

A review of the third subparagraph of Section 153
reveals that the Chairman is required to "[provide] for the
preparation and review of contingency plans which conform to
the policy guidance from the President and the Secretary of
Defense."[46]

13

This responsibility is clearly satisfied by the *Joint Strategic Capabilities Plan* (*JSCP*). While the *NMS* is an effective vehicle for the Chairman to assist the NCA in strategic direction and the *JSCP* is an effective tool to cause the CINCs to prepare contingency plans, neither fully attends to the Chairman's responsibility to prepare strategic plans.[47] One consequence of this planning lacuna is its negative effect on the development and implementation of joint doctrine.

Strategic plans should enumerate specific strategic objectives, identify constraints to include fiscal constraints, offer strategy for securing objectives, and should be key in determining force capability requirements.[48] They are envisaged to be comprehensive plans, based on a global perspective, that contain strategic priorities and strategies for attaining them.[49] These plans should set forth specific strategic concepts distilled from the broad general concepts presented in the *NMS*. These strategic concepts should help guide the development of joint doctrine. Therefore, the concepts must be specific if the derivative doctrine is to be useful in achieving the objectives outlined in the *NSS* and *NMS*.

An example helps illustrate this point. A *strategic concept* of the current *NMS* is *overseas presence*.[50] Along with *power projection*, this concept facilitates the three *components* of the strategy: *peacetime engagement, deterrence and conflict prevention,* and *fighting and winning our Nation's wars*.[51] One notes immediately that the *NMS* provides general definitions of overseas presence and peacetime engagement. It also describes them in terms of where forces are currently located and why they are there. For peacetime engagement, the strategy describes the different forms it may take and why it is important. The strategy is educational in that it informs the reader of the broad concepts and components of the *NMS* and why they are important. But there is nothing in the *NMS* that tells us *how* we should apply overseas presence to achieve the right type and amount of peacetime engagement, in the right places around the globe, to optimize the promotion of U.S. interests, given military capability (resource) limitations, for the period of time under consideration. However, these factors, and others, must be addressed if joint doctrine can be developed and linked to the broad, general concepts presented in the *NMS*.

Therefore, the value of strategic plans to the development of joint doctrine would be considerable. Not only would they provide the specific strategic concepts upon which joint doctrine should be based; more importantly, they would outline the contextual framework within which it would be developed. Additionally, strategic plans would provide a unifying mechanism for the services, CINCs, and defense agencies. This would:

• legitimize the preeminence of joint doctrine over individual service doctrines;

• result in better rationalized service doctrines;

• produce a more coherent body of joint doctrine; and,

• increase service predilection to implement joint doctrine.

In summary, neither the *NMS* nor the *JSCP* meets the requirements of strategic plans. The development of strategic plans, *inter alia*, would allow the services to arrive at a more common understanding of the *NMS* and a more unified commitment to a body of joint doctrine that would better support the *NMS*. Additionally, the applicability and implementation of joint doctrine at the theater level would be enhanced since contingency plans and joint doctrine would be *consistent* with an overarching strategic plan. In short, the direction provided by these documents would introduce a new rigor into strategic and operations planning, joint doctrine development and implementation, joint exercises, and joint operations. Interestingly, such a system already exists, in large part, in Australia.

Lessons from the Antipodes.

Developments over the past 25 years in the Australian Department of Defence and the Australian Defence Force (ADF) provide many useful lessons on threat-benign, as well as top-down, defense planning. Beginning in the early 1970s,

Australia no longer formally used "threats" as the basis for its defense planning, and later initiated a number of reforms to effect a stronger degree of jointness throughout the ADF. This section will not dwell at length on the Australian defense planning system, as this subject has already been documented and analyzed elsewhere.[52] What will be presented is a précis of Australia's defense planning methodology and how strategic guidance is conveyed through the planning system for execution and for the development of joint doctrine, which from all accounts is actively *used*.[53]

Defense planning in Australia begins with the government's current defense white paper,[54] a document that provides policy and strategy much in the same way that the *NSS* and *NMS* do in the U.S. system. Strategic guidance for the ADF is further refined by strategic planning documents.[55] Second, a net assessment of the military capabilities of other regional states is derived, without consideration given to their intent to employ their capabilities against Australia. Third, "credible contingencies" are developed which provide a baseline of regional military capabilities, against which the Department of Defence conducts capabilities planning. Fourth, projected financial guidance is provided to enable force development planners to produce force structure priorities.

The above planning system is somewhat unique in that it is not threat-based. Prescient for the purposes of this essay, is that Australian strategic guidance is employed to develop "Strategic Concepts."[56] These important principles outline the missions that the ADF is likely to be required to perform. These are national level strategic concepts and are not comparable to regional strategic concepts developed by U.S. combatant commanders, nor can they be equated to more specific concepts found in U.S. joint doctrine.

Australian Strategic Concepts provide a very useful foundation for the development of the ADF's joint doctrine. They consist of specified task parameters (e.g., rates of effort, location, and duration), and judgements of task priorities (where possible). Strategic Concepts have become the prime influence in the Australian force development process in recent years. In fact, it is extremely difficult for a service to propose obtaining new equipment or capabilities unless the service can show that they would directly support an existing Strategic Concept.[57] A strong relationship also exists between Strategic Concepts and joint doctrine.

Joint doctrine is viewed by the ADF as essential in ensuring that the ADF is capable of performing the missions described by Strategic Concepts. The ADF Warfare Centre, established in 1990, is chartered to develop and teach joint doctrine, manage the ADF exercise analyses plan and maintain an analytical data base for post-exercise analyses.[58] The Centre concerns itself with developing and validating joint doctrine at the operational level of warfare.[59] Generally, the Centre does not participate in the development of tactical level doctrine. This is left to the individual services, but it must be developed in accordance with joint doctrine.

Joint doctrine has come to play an important role in the activities of the ADF in recent years for a variety of important reasons. First, as a result of a series of command reorganizations,[60] the ADF, perforce, has had to become more proficient in joint operations. Consequently, ADF exercises are now *always* joint. Joint doctrine, such as *Australian Defence Force Publication (ADFP) 1 "Doctrine,"* has become umbrella guidance for the three services, to which their service doctrines *must* conform.[61] The services have come to accept joint doctrine as a very useful means to achieve the often illusive goal of "jointness." Second, and perhaps more important, a key objective of joint doctrine is to help translate Strategic Concepts into operational directives. In this respect, joint doctrine flows from and supports the specific concepts. Thus, ADF joint doctrine provides the methods by which the services can support Australian national strategy.[62] Although the services previously found it difficult individually to demonstrate that they were capable of executing Strategic Concepts, joint doctrine now provides important and necessary integrating and rationalizing guidance.[63] Third, by providing guidance requisite to achieving Strategic Concepts, ADF joint doctrine assists the ADF's three environmental and one geographic commanders. It helps them to assess and demonstrate their commands' preparedness to accomplish missions as stipulated in the

Headquarters ADF's *Master Task List*, as well as to respond to the *Chief of Defence Force's Preparedness Directive* (which establishes readiness levels in the ADF).[64]

ADF joint doctrinal development accomplishes these ambitious objectives in the following manner. First, joint teams of field grade officers with recent operational experience draft doctrine at the ADF Warfare Centre. Within this process, *it is a truism that for joint doctrine to be valid, it must address Strategic Concepts*. Once completed and vetted by Centre staff, joint doctrine is reviewed for approval by an organization called the Joint Operations Doctrine Group. This group is comprised of representatives from the three services, the joint commands, Headquarters ADF, and other interested parties. Draft doctrine is subsequently staffed through the service staffs. Agreement on publication is reached through consensus. The watering down effect that consensus-building produces during the development of U.S. joint doctrine is largely mitigated during the development of ADF joint doctrine, because its focus on Strategic Concepts is assured during the early stages of development and maintained throughout the coordination phase.

Joint doctrine is evaluated and validated through the ADF Warfare Centre's regular observation of joint and combined exercises to ensure that joint doctrine is both relevant and workable. The Assistant Chief of Defence Force (operations) sponsors these visits, thereby ensuring Headquarters ADF's involvement in the review process. Observed doctrinal inadequacies could result in a review of existing doctrine. In this manner, the ADF endeavors to ensure that doctrine remains relevant and useful to operators in the field. Knowledge of joint doctrine is disseminated in large part through a large number of courses conducted annually by the ADF Warfare Centre; training of ADF personnel is one of its key functions.[65]

Assessment.

This analysis does not advocate that the Australian defense planning system and the ADF's joint doctrine models be adopted by the U.S. Department of Defense. There are obvious and significant dissimilarities of scale. Nevertheless, the Australian system's methodologies and the crucial linkage between Australian strategic planning and joint doctrine offer insights into improving U.S. joint doctrine development and encouraging its implementation. The Australian system demonstrates that it is possible to have a strategic planning system and joint doctrine development process that integrate to provide a coherent logic-flow from national security policy, to strategic guidance, to strategic planning, and to joint doctrine development and implementation.

Applying the pertinent features of the Australian systems to the U.S. strategic planning and joint doctrine processes suggests the Joint Staff should develop strategic plans to provide a more coherent linkage between the *NMS* and the operation planning of the CINCs. Analogous to the manner in which theater operation plans develop and elaborate on the strategic concepts found in CINCs' theater strategies, national level strategic plans would present the specific concepts that would not only unify the planning efforts of the various CINCs, but would elaborate on, and add meaning to, the broader concepts presented in the *NMS*.[66] Furthermore, the unifying effect of strategic plans would provide an overarching framework that would promote a common understanding within DoD of the broad and general concepts set forth in the *NMS*. Strategic plans would also provide authoritative and specific guidance for use in developing agreed upon, rationalized, and practicable joint doctrine. The responsiveness of joint doctrine to the *NMS* could be enhanced and it would be less influenced by parochialism of the Lead Agent. This would be accomplished by ensuring that early drafts of joint doctrine are consistent with strategic plans. The U.S. Joint Warfighting Center should be assigned that responsibility.

Additionally, if in the course of doctrine development services are unable to reach agreement on certain doctrinal issues, the Joint Warfighting Center, on behalf of the Chairman, could base its arbitration of the dispute on the strategic concepts contained in the strategic plans. While perhaps not perfect, the adoption of these methodologies would significantly improve the Department of Defense's development and implementation of joint doctrine while bringing the U.S. armed forces closer to effecting the intent of the Goldwater-Nichols Act.

Conclusion.

This essay has argued that improvements in U.S. joint doctrine development and implementation are required and can be accomplished, in part, through improvement in strategic planning. This can also result in a more coherent translation of the broad concepts of the *NMS* for the combatant commands and services, leading to improved operation planning. Certainly, the changes outlined above and recommended below, although controversial, have sufficient merit to warrant further examination. A strategic planning system that makes the U.S. armed forces more responsive to the *NMS* could have significant systemic implications. By making joint doctrine more responsive to the *NMS* and requiring service doctrine to conform to it, service and joint training and exercises would be better focused and harmonized. Ultimately, the CINCs would be provided forces better prepared to accomplish their assigned missions.

This essay, however, does not imply that the Chairman has been unaware of the need to improve joint doctrine development and implementation. For example, the key initiative started by General Colin Powell and consummated by General John Shalikashvili, the combination of the Joint Doctrine Center with the Joint Warfare Center to form the aforementioned Joint Warfighting Center, created an organization that will, *inter alia*, take a more active role in the development of joint doctrine. This reform should reduce problems inherent in the current joint doctrine development process. Capitalizing on its potential, the new center has the potential to ensure that publications are truly joint in their early stages of development. This could be accomplished in at least two ways. One alternative would be for the Joint Warfighting Center to organize and manage inter-service joint doctrine development teams, thus obviating the need for Lead Agents. A more preferable alternative might include retention of the

Lead Agent practice, however; the Joint Warfighting Center would provide authoritative guidance and resolve issues on behalf of the Chairman throughout the joint doctrine development process. Either alternative would enable the Joint Warfighting Center to form early consensus on joint doctrine issues and ensure that doctrine is void of any bias toward a particular service from the beginning.[67]

Another major initiative taken by the Chairman is the more effectual dissemination of joint doctrine throughout the U.S. armed forces. Concerned that forces provided by the services do not apply joint doctrine because of a general lack of familiarity and understanding, the Chairman has directed the review and revision, if necessary, of all existing joint doctrine publications. Moreover, by using a multi-media approach, the Joint Staff hopes to make the doctrine more accessible, readable, and understandable.[68]

These examples evince the Chairman's desire to effect reforms to improve joint doctrine development and implementation. However, a promising reform yet to be implemented is the development of strategic plans and ensuring that they guide the development of joint doctrine. In an era of strategic ambiguity and defense penury, the need for U.S. forces to be as effectively and efficiently responsive to the *NMS* as possible has never been greater.

Recommendations.

- Strategic plans, as envisaged by the Goldwater-Nichols Act, should be developed to add definition and utility to the *NMS* and provide the specific strategic concepts upon which joint doctrine should be based.

- The service doctrine centers and the newly created Joint Warfighting Center should move toward closer coordination and greater integration.

- The concept of Lead Agency should be modified to ensure that the Joint Warfighting Center assumes a more assertive role in managing joint doctrine development.

• The Chairman should clarify and emphasize his policy that joint doctrine is authoritative.

• The Chairman should implement a process that ensures that service doctrine conforms to, and is consistent with, joint doctrine.

• The Australian Defence Forces' joint doctrine development methodology should be studied for possible applications within the U.S. armed forces joint doctrine development process.

ENDNOTES

1. U.S. Congress, Senate, Committee on Armed Services, *Defense Organization and the Need for Change,* Staff Report, 99th Congress, 1st Session, Washington, DC: U.S. Government Printing office, 1985, p. 1; and, U.S. Congress, House of Representatives, *Goldwater-Nichols Department of Defense Reorganization Act of 1986,* Report 99-824, 99th Congress, 2nd Session, Washington, DC: U.S. Government Printing office, 1986, p. 3.

2. U.S. Congress, House of Representatives, Committee on Armed Services, *Title 10, United States Code, Armed Forces*, 103rd Congress, 1st Session, Washington, DC: U.S. Government Printing Office, April 1993, Section 155.

3. U.S. Department of Defense, Chairman Joint Chiefs of Staff, *National Military Strategy of the United States of America: Strategy of Flexible and Selective Engagement,* Washington, DC, February 1995, pp. 1-20.

4. The strategic concepts envisaged here differ from the broad concepts found in the *National Security Strategy, National Military Strategy* and other national strategic planning documents. These strategic concepts would be sufficiently specific and focused to help form the basis for developing new, and reviewing existing, joint doctrine. Many factors, including historical writings, legislation, operational experience, and technological developments, combined with strategic planning, form a multidimensional basis for the establishment of joint doctrine. This essay focuses on the strategic planning dimension.

5. The White House, *A National Security Strategy of Engagement and Enlargement,* Washington, DC, February 1995, pp. 1-33.

6. John Boatman, "Spreading the Word," *Jane's Defence Weekly*, December 10, 1994, p. 19.

7. On behalf of the Chairman of the Joint Chiefs of the Staff, the Director of the Joint Staff issued on July 28, 1994 a memorandum (MCM-90-94) to all Service Chiefs and Unified Combatant Commanders-in-Chief regarding joint doctrine. In this memorandum the Chairman directed that the doctrinal concept found in the preface of all joint publications be changed.

8. U.S. Department of Defense, Office of the Chairman of the Joint Chiefs of Staff, *Joint Pub 1-01: Joint Publication System, Joint Doctrine and Joint Tactics, Techniques, and Procedures Development Program*, Washington, DC, July 30, 1992, pp. I-1 thru III-15.

9. See, for example, U.S. Department of Defense, Chairman of the Joint Chiefs of Staff, *Joint Pub 1: Joint Warfare of the US Armed Forces,* Washington, DC: U.S. Government Printing Office, January 1995.

10. Arthur F. Lykke, "Toward an Understanding of Military Strategy," in *Military Strategy: Theory and Application,* ed. by Arthur F. Lykke, Carlisle Barracks: U.S. Army War College, May 1, 1986, p. 3.

11. *Joint Pub 1: Joint Warfare of the US Armed Forces,* p. I-3; U.S. Department of Defense, Chairman of the Joint Chiefs of Staff, *Joint Pub 0-2, Unified Action Armed Forces (UNAAF)*, Washington, DC, p. vi; and, U.S. Department of Defense, Chairman of the Joint Chiefs of Staff, *Joint Pub 3-0, Doctrine for Joint Operations*, Washington, DC, February 1, 1995, p. I-1.

12. See, U.S. Department of Defense, Chairman of the Joint Chiefs of Staff, *User's Guide for JOPES (Joint Operation Planning and Execution System)*, Washington, DC, May 1, 1995, p. 9.

13. We acknowledge the proviso in *Joint Pub 1-01* (p. I-2) that "Joint doctrine will be written to reflect extant capabilities." However, we consider it to be superficial with respect to the proper relationship between joint doctrine and force capability development. Obviously, the Department of Defense would not develop military capabilities and then try to ascertain how best to use them. Alternatively, the joint doctrine development process should consider potential force capability development options. To say that joint doctrine must be written to reflect extant capabilities ignores the dynamic and reciprocating relationship between joint doctrine and force capability development.

14. *Joint Pub 1-01,* pp. I-1 thru I-2.

15. *Title 10, United States Code, Armed Forces,* section 153 (a) (5).

16. *Ibid.*

17. There has been renewed criticism of the Chairman's management of joint training. See U.S. Government Accounting Office, *Military Capabilities: Stronger Joint Staff Needed to Enhance Joint Military Training,* Report NSIAD-95-109, Washington, DC, July 6, 1995.

18. U.S. Department of Defense, Chairman of the Joint Chiefs of Staff, *Military Education Policy Document*, CM-1618-93, Washington, DC, March 23, 1993, Chapter 3 and Appendix A.

19. *Title 10, United States Code, Armed Forces,* sections 153(a)(4) and 163 (b)(2).

20. U.S. Department of Defense, Chairman of the Joint Chiefs of Staff, *Report on the Roles, Missions, and Functions of the Armed Forces of the United States,* CM-1584-93, Washington, DC: U.S. Government Printing Office, February 10, 1993, pp. II-18/19; III-15/16; and, III-37.

21. Bradley Graham, "Air Force Chief on Attack: McPeak Boldly Criticizes other Services' Roles and Plans," *Washington Post,* October 24, 1994, p. 1; and GEN Merrill McPeak, USAF, Chief of Staff, U.S. Air Force, briefing given before the Roles and Mission Commission, Washington, DC, September 14, 1994.

22. U.S. Department of Defense, Chairman of the Joint Chiefs of Staff, *Universal Joint Task List,* CJCSM 3500.04, Version 2.1, Washington, DC, May 15, 1995.

23. Lewis D. Eigen and Jonathan P. Siegel, *Macmillan Dictionary of Political Quotations,* New York: Macmillan Publishing Company, 1993, p. 325.

24. John Boatman, "The Jane's Interview," *Jane's Defense Weekly*, December 10, 1994, p. 32.

25. *Idem*, "Spreading the Word," *Jane's Defense Weekly*, December 10, 1994, p. 19.

26. The use of the double-negative here is intentional. Service concurrence on a piece of joint doctrine may mean agreement but more often than not merely means the service does not strongly disagree with it.

27. Michael J. Morin, Professor of Doctrine at the U.S. Army War College, has conducted a comprehensive review of current joint doctrine. He discovered a considerable number of areas of substantial internal inconsistency and numerous others of lesser significance. The Joint Staff

J-7 Joint Doctrine Division and the Joint Warfighting Center are dealing with these problems.

28. U.S. Department of Defense, Office of the Chairman of the Joint Chiefs of Staff, *Joint Pub 1-02: Department of Defense Dictionary of Military and Associated Terms,* Washington, DC: U.S. Government Printing Office, March 23, 1994, p. 120.

29. U.S. Department of the Army, *U.S. Army Field Manual 100-1: The Army,* Washington, DC: U.S. Government Printing Office, June 1994, "Foreword."

30. On behalf of the Chairman of the Joint Chiefs of the Staff, the Director of the Joint Staff issued on July 28, 1994 a memorandum to all Service Chiefs and Unified Combatant Commanders-in-Chief regarding joint doctrine. In this memorandum the Chairman directed that the applicability paragraph found in the preface of all joint publications be changed to read: "The guidance in this publication is authoritative; as such, commanders will apply this doctrine (JTTP) except when exceptional circumstances dictate otherwise." In a September 15, 1994 memorandum the Commander of the U.S. Army Training and Doctrine Command wrote that the Chairman's ". . . views are consistent with the Army view that doctrine is authoritative, but requires judgement in application." While the Commander of TRADOC acknowledged doctrine to be authoritative, he appeared to endorse the exercise of "judgement and application" for situations with less than "exceptional circumstances."

31. In a February 8, 1995 memorandum to the Commission on Roles and Missions of the Armed Forces, Air Force Major General Link expressed the Air Force's concern that "Current Joint doctrine is largely dominated by outmoded perspectives which handcuff airpower to the constrained mission of land component commanders." Additionally, an analysis of Appendix H of *Joint Pub 1-01* reveals that the Army has been designated Lead Agent significantly more often than the Air Force and almost twice as often as the Navy and Marine Corps combined.

32. James J. Tritten and Gary W. Anderson, "Lessons from the History of Naval Doctrine Development," *Marine Corps Gazette,* Vol. 78, No. 10, October 1994, pp. 50-52. In response to criticism that the Navy's use of doctrine has been spotty at best, the recently created Naval Doctrine Command held forth a number of historical documents as containing past or current doctrine. This was not very convincing proof of past emphasis on formal doctrine.

33. U.S. Department of the Navy, Office of the Chief of Naval operations, *Naval Doctrine Publication 1: Naval Warfare,* Washington, DC, March 28, 1994.

34. *Ibid.*

35. Carl Builder, *The Masks of War*, Baltimore: The Johns Hopkins University Press, 1989, pp. 18-30.

36. U.S. Marine Corps, *Warfighting, Fleet Marine Force Manual 1*, March 6, 1989, pp. 43-44.

37. *Joint Pub 1-01*, pp. II-2 thru II-3.
38. *Ibid*, p. I-2.

39. U.S. Department of the Army, *Army Focus 93*, Washington, DC: U.S. Army Publication and Printing Command, September 1993, pp. 29-30.

40. *Title 10, United States Code, Armed Forces,* section 155 (e).

41. In a July 28, 1994 memorandum (CM-378-94) to all the Service Chiefs and Combatant Commanders-in-Chief, the CJCS, in response to the accidental downing of the U.S. Army helicopters, directed their "immediate and serious attention" to specific elements of joint doctrine: Command and Control for Joint Air Operations and JTTP for Close Air Support.

42. *Joint Pub 1, Joint Warfare of the US Armed Forces,* p. I-3.

43. *Title 10, United States Code, Armed Forces,* section 153(a)(1).

44. U.S., *National Military Strategy, passim*; and, see our essay, *U.S. Department of Defense Strategic Planning: The Missing Nexus,* Carlisle Barracks, PA: Strategic Studies Institute, September 1, 1995, *passim.*

45. *Title 10, United States Code, Armed Forces,* section 153(a)(2).

46. *Ibid.*, section 153(a)(3).

47. Office of the Chairman of the Joint Chiefs of Staff, *Instructional Joint Strategic Capabilities Plan,* MCM-126-92, Washington, DC, August 25, 1992. A review of the *Instructional JSCP* shows that it provides a précis of the *NMS*, general planning guidance to the CINCs and the services, assigns specific, regionally focused, planning tasks to the CINCs, and lists and apportions forces for planning. Of particular note is what the *JSCP* does not provide. It does not assign missions, nor does it provide national level integration of the planning efforts of the various CINCs. Therefore, it cannot be considered a strategic plan within the context of *10 USC*, section 153.

48. U.S. Congress, *Defense Organization and the Need for Change,* pp. 493-500. See, as well, *U.S. Department of Defense Strategic Planning.*

49. *Title 10 United States Code, Armed Forces*, sections 153(a)(3)(C), 153(a)(4)(B), 153(a)(4)(E).

50. *National Military Strategy,* p. 6.

51. Although a similar argument could be made for the other two components, for brevity we will analyze peacetime engagement only. Of the two concepts, overseas presence is more applicable to peacetime engagement, so we will use it for our illustrative analysis.

52. See Paul Dibb, *The Conceptual Basis of Australia's Defence Planning and Force Structure Development,* Canberra Papers on Strategy and Defence No. 88, Canberra: Strategic and Defence Studies Centre, Australian National University, 1992; and, Thomas-Durell Young, *Threat-Ambiguous Defense Planning: The Australian Experience*, Carlisle Barracks, PA: Strategic Studies Institute, September 10, 1993.

53. Interviews with numerous ADF operational commanders in Canberra, ACT, Holsworthy, NSW, Sydney, NSW, and Newcastle, NSW, December 1994.

54. Australia, Department of Defence, *Defending Australia: Defence White Paper 1994,* Canberra: Australian Government Publishing Service, 1994.

55. For example, Australia, Department of Defence, *Strategic Review December 1993*, Canberra, Defence Central, 1993.

56. These are essentially listed in *ibid.,* Annex, pp. 61-67.

57. Discussion with Australian defense officials, Russell Offices, Canberra, ACT, December 1994.

58. The Australian Defence Force Warfare Centre was created on July 1, 1990 through an amalgamation of the Australian Joint Warfare Establishment and the Australian Joint Maritime Warfare Centre. Personal correspondence from Colonel D. J. Murray, Australian Defence Force Warfare Centre, April 25, 1995.

59. There is, in actuality, very little in the published literature on the Australian Defence Force Warfare Centre. One of the few essays which provide general information and the historical development of joint warfighting doctrine in Australia is, Al Clancy, "Australian Defence Force Warfare Centre, *Maritime Patrol Aviation: The Voice of VP International*, Volume 2, No. 4, March 1993, pp. 18-21.

60. See, *Report on the Implementation of the Structural Review of Higher ADF Staff Arrangements,* Canberra, Directorate of Departmental Publications Division, Management Improvement and Manpower Policy Division, May 1, 1990.

61. *ADFP 1, "Doctrine,"* November 30, 1993, paragraph 110.

62. See, for example, *ADFP 6 "Operations" (Interim Edition)*, draft, December 1994.

63. *ADFP 1, "Doctrine,"* Chapter 2, "Functions and Roles of the ADF."

64. Briefings, Australian Defence Force Warfare Centre, RAAF Base Williamtown, NSW, December 1994.

65. Briefing Charts, "Australian Defence Force Warfare Centre," May 1994; and, personal correspondence from Colonel D. J. Murray, Australian Defence Force Warfare Centre, November 2, 1994.

66. U.S. Department of Defense, Chairman of the Joint Chiefs of Staff, *Joint Operation Planning and Execution System, Volume I, Planning Policies and Procedures, Joint Pub 5-03.1,* Washington, DC, August 4, 1993, III-1/III-12. Our use of the term "operation plan" conforms to the JOPES discussion of operation planning contained in this Joint Pub. We recognize that deliberate operation plans may be further developed into theater campaign plans.

67. John Boatmen, p. 19.

68. *Ibid.*

U.S. ARMY WAR COLLEGE

Major General Richard A. Chilcoat
Commandant

* * * * *

STRATEGIC STUDIES INSTITUTE

Director
Colonel Richard H. Witherspoon

Director of Research
Dr. Earl H. Tilford, Jr.

Authors
DDouglas C. Lovelace, Jr.
Thomas-Durell Young

Editor
Mrs. Marianne P. Cowling

Secretaries
Mrs. Shirley E. Martin
Ms. Rita A. Rummel
Mrs. Kay L. Williams

* * * * *

Composition
Mrs. Mary Jane Semple

Cover Artist
Mr. James E. Kistler

www.ingramcontent.com/pod-product-compliance
Lightning Source LLC
Chambersburg PA
CBHW082245310526
45795CB00014B/2753